What I Didn't Post on Instagram: A Collection of Essays on Real Lives And What We Filter Out

Edited By
Chrissy Stockton

THOUGHT
CATALOG
Books

Collective
World

This book was designed by KJ Parish and published by Thought
Catalog Books, a publishing house owned by The Thought &
Expression Company. It was printed in the United States and
was published in an edition of 1,000 copies.

ISBN 978-1-945796-63-0

For messy women
who don't pretend to
have it all figured out.

Introduction

by Chrissy Stockton

I am not a yogi. I can do, like, max four breaths in downward dog before my arms start to tap out. I can't shift my body into most positions (all of which I've learned about solely from watching yoga on YouTube instead of going to classes, because I'm a baby who's intimidated by the latter). I'm even bad at mindfulness; I can't tell you the last time I let myself fall asleep without a combination of melatonin and Netflix so that I can ensure I'm not going to be alone with my thoughts for even a minute.

But I had a rough winter. Out of nowhere I was having anxiety and depression-related thoughts I hadn't dealt with in a similar intensity for a decade. Nothing "happened"—I had a great job, I had a lot of people who inexplicably cared about me enough to listen to me cry on the phone for however long I wanted, and there'd been no changes in my health or relationship status. Every exterior thing in my life was the same as it had been during some of the best times in my life, but my happiness and sanity had decided to take a nosedive nonetheless.

This is how I found myself in a car making a six-hour trek to a YMCA camp near the Minnesota-Canadian border with an acquaintance who told me about a yoga retreat she thought I'd love. I knew most of the people going would be really into yoga and I'd probably feel stupid a lot, but my mental health had taken such a beating I was willing to make an idiot out of myself if it helped me feel better.

We stopped at a few places on the way and took beautiful photos of Lake Superior and snowy roads in the north woods and I immediately uploaded them to Instagram. I was play-acting that I was like all the other chill yogis on Insta, one with nature and so obviously Zen—someone who had things figured out. There was a bit of a disconnect when the comments rolled in: "You're always on vacation," one read. I guess most of my friends didn't know that this was sort of a last resort for me. That I was really doing this because I honestly didn't know what was going to happen if I couldn't get some relief from my anxious brain in the very near future. I knew how it must look like a "vacation" from the outside, but I was still surprised that anyone could think my sloppy, weak little life was glamorous.

At the retreat, we holed up in beautiful little cabins with five to six strangers each and would attend a session each morning and afternoon which consisted of an hour of yogi teachings, an hour of yoga practice, and an hour of writing exercises. There was a lot of crying!!!! I cried constantly on this trip. I cried at first circle time when we had to share our reason for coming and I had to talk about what a mental-ward reject I felt like lately. I cried during yoga practice when I felt dumb for not being able to do anything right. I cried during writing exercises when we had to do extremely bleak (but helpful!) stuff like write our eulogies as if we died right now and how our failure to achieve our dharma (the purpose you're alive to fulfill) has affected our friends, families, and ourselves. Fun stuff! I also cried back at my cabin as I bonded with my cabinmates and explained things about myself such as how I hate that I'm always crying.

I was beaten down and out of my carefully preserved comfort zone. Memorably, I got up from one session and walked back to our cabin alone so I could seethe quietly and scream, "This is BULLSHIT" over and over in my head. I was skeptical from the beginning because there is a lot of money to be made in telling people you can change their lives for the better—we're all holding our collective breath for a magic pill that's going to take all our existential pain away—so I'm suspicious of everyone who tries to sell me the answers I am still desperately seeking. But I went home and read more from the book we were supposed to read and tried to open my mind and open my heart and remember that nothing was going to hurt me at the very worst. Everything could only help, even if I later realized it was made up. It could do the trick temporarily. I did all the work we were supposed to do, even if sometimes I did it as an angry skeptic who thinks maybe the whole thing is set up by grifters.

I expected to feel something because I'm a sensitive person and things set up to make you feel something usually work on me (have you not read about all the crying?). But I didn't expect to have the kind of A-HA! moments I had after a particularly tense afternoon where I had to list all my negative behaviors and work on figuring out the unconscious desires that compelled me to act this way. (Example would be, "My desire to avoid or immediately quell bad feelings motivates me to avoid situations where I am alone with my thoughts by constantly listening to music/engaging with text/scrolling through my phone like a deranged teen girl.") I put some things together and as someone who always likes a nice juicy explanation, understanding the "why" of some of the thoughts and behaviors that had made my winter so rough felt good, productive. There was something I could work with here.

In our last session on the morning we were all going home, I struggled through our practice per usual, but we did a very long (maybe 30 minutes) meditation and I enjoyed it! And my mind didn't wander away to think about how awful I think I am! I felt chill and calm and enjoyed imagining a little almond of fire inside my navel like the instructor told me to. It was mid-morning so all this hot sunlight was coming in through the windows and onto my closed eyes and I kept pretending I was so good at meditation that I was making the whole room hot.

We circled up and talked about what we learned over the course of the retreat. I watched how gracefully everyone got up to retrieve their carefully chosen sacred objects from the altar at the front of the room and then felt embarrassed when I rolled around and walked over to get the bougie piece of jewelry I'd decided to use. I told everyone I'd learned that there could be space between me and my problems. I didn't have to feel like I was in a mania just because there was some unhappiness or dis-ease bubbling below my surface. I could acknowledge unhappiness and work on it without being consumed by it instead of continuing to hope for this impossible thing, which is that I reach some fictional Zen point and never experience unhappiness again.

I came home and did *Yoga With Adriene* on YouTube before bed and again in the morning. The next day, back at work, I sat itching as the sun came out. I closed my laptop and walked around a lake. I went to bed without my phone and without melatonin. I woke up in the morning and felt good and then meditated anyway.

I'm not saying I'm fixed (fun fact: I'm not!!) or healed or anything. But I got some good medicine. I didn't become a perfect Instagram yogi; I became one who still has sad winters and dark nights of the soul, and I can learn to live with this.

I think if I did yoga and meditated daily I would feel better daily. I worry about it because I am worried about tricking myself into thinking something is a magic pill—and a good indicator for that is that you have to do it all the time in order for it to work.

But maybe—and this is a working hypothesis—instead of worrying I am being tricked by a medicine you take once and then are magically healed by, I can consider that gardens require maintenance. Fallible human beings require maintenance. There is weeding and watering to be done every day, and there's never a point where you are done working and your garden suddenly takes care of itself.

Maybe I am a shitty little garden whose gardener thought gardening books were bullshit, I don't know!

But it feels good to feel better; even if it's just a temporary reprieve, it's worth being embarrassed because you can't press your palms into your mat in forward fold. I don't know if all those other yogis' brains are better than mine, calmer and full of self-love and acceptance. They certainly look that way on the outside, the way my trip photos did to the people who didn't know what I was doing up north to begin with. It looked like I had it all together, it looked like I was on vacation—how would they know any better?

What I didn't post on Instagram was how low I felt when I was taking all those pictures. I didn't post about how desperate I was to feel better. I didn't post that even though all that yoga helped, I was also learning that nothing is magic. I was learning that there is never going to be a way to get rid of my unhappiness completely, but a better goal can be to learn to take space from it and to coexist with it in a more peaceful way.

·······

I originally published a version of this essay on Thought Catalog in February 2016, a week or so after I returned from my trip. Something spiritual happened as I was putting the words together on the screen. The less I tried to make things look good, the more brutally open I was about the dysfunction I was experiencing, the better I felt. Weights were lifted off of me. People wrote to me to tell me that reading it helped them. Some of them had failed to become perfect Instagram yogis, too, and were more drawn to the idea of being one who still has to tend to their garden every day. That seemed more manageable, more real.

All the painful honesty was cathartic for everyone. My life was a mess—and it still was, yoga or no yoga. Every time I post an idyllic update on a social media network, you can be sure that my monkey brain is also in attendance, telling me things to feel insecure about and generally being a fuck-up. I don't know if this is true for everyone, but I do know it's overwhelmingly true for the women I know and we do best by ourselves when we pull back the curtain a little bit and let everyone comparing their everyday to our highlight reel know that we struggle, too. Our happily ever afters contain some unhappiness, too.

This book is a collection of essays from women who are offering just that: the real moments that accompany the surreal ones.

None of these stories is a before-and-after makeover. No one is going to use the second-person writing voice to tell you how you can be as happy as they are as long as you both swallow the same kind of green juice. This is a messy and imperfect assembly of women learning out loud that we can be proud of the milestones and curated experiences we share with our friends on social media, but that there is real power in acknowledging the human moments we don't post, too.

In Which the Emergency Room Nurse Compliments My Engagement Ring

by Kim Quindlen

After holding it in my chest all morning, I finally let out a strangled, pathetic little sob into my hospital bed pillow. A second, pathetic little sob followed suit.

For a moment, I was distracted by how weird and pitiful the noise was as it came out of my mouth. It was almost funny how dramatic it all seemed; combined with the weird fetal position I was in, I felt like I was a bad actor on an episode of *Grey's Anatomy*. Eventually I looked up and saw Sean staring at me, his eyes wet.

"What?" I said, panicked.

He cleared his throat. His voice came out low and scratchy, like always. "It's just hard for me to see you in pain and to know that I can't do anything."

We had probably been waiting to see a doctor for an hour or two. Or, I don't know, maybe it was seventeen. When you're in the waiting room of the ER and in extreme pain, every minute feels insanely long.

Finally (after securing our $250 copay) they led us into a curtained-off area where I was able to curl sideways on a bed while we waited for someone, anyone, to come help us.

After I was diagnosed twelve years ago, this was the first time that Crohn's Disease had taken me as far as the emergency room. I had some close calls in the past—plenty of bad days, plenty of bad weeks, and some Very Bad Months where the inflammation in my body was so bad that I could barely eat anything or do anything. Dark circles under my eyes from exhaustion, collarbones jutting out from my chest due to losing weight so unnaturally fast, running to the bathroom every few minutes after eating just *one* wrong thing—all those sexy symptoms.

If you're unfamiliar with Crohn's Disease, I will explain it very quickly in regular-people terms: My digestive system is chronically inflamed, so my day-to-day life involves consistent abdominal pain, frequent diarrhea, an inability to digest many foods, constant anxiety that comes directly from the unpredictability of my body, and lots of other fun surprises like going to the ER on a busy Monday morning.

Eventually we heard footsteps on the other side of the curtain. Sean let out a fast, heavy breath. He squeezed my hand. "They're here, I think. You'll be okay now."

The doctor came in and asked all the fun doctory questions: *Where do you feel the worst pain? Have you eaten anything unusual in the last few days? When was your last bowel movement? Can you describe your last bowel movement?* I murmured my answers while Sean rubbed my hand with his thumb and looked at the ground, knowing that I felt awkward having to talk about all of this in front of him.

They were concerned about a stomach obstruction, which is apparently very serious. They did an X-ray. It wasn't that. Eventually, they determined that the problem stemmed from the fact that I had taken Imodium several days before and my body reacted poorly to it—as in, I hadn't gone to the bathroom in six days and because my gastrointestinal tract was already such a mess, this just added fuel to the fire. This was where all the pain was coming from.

The doctor then had to do what I will scientifically refer to as a "butt exam," which was the last thing I wanted to happen while I was still clutching my stomach in pain. I asked Sean to stand outside the curtain. This whole experience was humiliating enough that I didn't need him to be in there during *this* part of it, too. The doctor began the exam and a nurse held my left hand while I let out more pathetic little sobs. "That's a pretty ring," she said, nodding to my finger. "Are you having fun planning the wedding?"

"Sure, it's fine," I choked out. She was trying to be sweet, to get me to talk about something happy in order to distract me. Instead, I cried. The talk of my upcoming wedding, as exciting as it normally was, didn't bring me any comfort in this moment. The morphine they eventually gave me certainly did, though.

When it was all over, Sean came back into the room, working hard to keep his face neutral. Later, we would get home and he would immediately pour a large glass of wine and tell me that standing on the other side of the curtain and hearing me in that sort of pain was something he didn't want to hear ever again.

I write about these experiences often in my work. I try to be fairly open about the struggles, the anxieties, the embarrassing aspects of my illness.

My Instagram, on the other hand, tells a different story. It tells this story:

I am engaged to someone who makes me feel joyful and silly and loved. I am a full-time staff writer for Thought Catalog and am living in the heart of Chicago. I spend my days writing in bright, beautiful cafes. I spend my nights performing improv and sketch comedy all over a city that is considered the mecca of comedy. I travel to fascinating cities to visit wonderful friends. I am very happy with where I am; I am very happy with who I am.

These things are all true. They are not lies that I'm trying to craft in order to display *the perfect life.*

But what I like to remember when I'm overwhelmed with the glamorous nightlife or adorable relationships or bougie living spaces of other people I follow online is that my Instagram looks like that, too—vibrant, exciting, joy-filled, cool.

Those pieces of me that I share with the world are genuine. I'm doing those things. I'm getting married to that wonderful guy. I'm performing comedy on that stage. But those photos don't include every little piece that makes up each of those "happy" truths.

There's a photo of me tagged on Instagram with my improv team, looking spirited and excited and overjoyed, because we had just broken the record number of wins for a well-known performance competition in the community. It shows me up on stage bright-eyed, chasing my dream, doing something incredibly scary and incredibly thrilling. What it doesn't show is that I had spent the hours leading up to it running in and out of the bathroom, my stomach horribly upset from something I had eaten, with the adrenaline of my upcoming show only making everything worse. In the moments before we ran onstage, I clutched my stomach, rocking from foot to foot, barely able to breathe, hoping I would last the whole show without having to run offstage and go right to the bathroom. I took an Imodium that night in order to even be able to leave the house and do the thing that I loved. And then six days later, I ended up in the emergency room because of it. That's the part that is not included in the caption of that picture or any of the others—because there's a lot of those, a lot of pictures of incredible nights onstage that were preceded by fourteen trips to the bathroom in a matter of two or three hours.

There's a photo on my Instagram of Sean and I from last summer, announcing our engagement and appearing filled with joy, because we were. There are a lot of photos on my Instagram that look like that— me with a person who makes me laugh and loves me deeply and makes my life seem very romantic.

That's all true, too. I really am happy and in love. But those photos will never encapsulate those moments in the ER while I sweated in an ugly hospital gown and made unattractively pained faces and had to talk about my bowel movements in front of my fiancé.

Sometimes when we vent about Instagram, we like to talk about it in a way where it seems like everything that everybody posts is bullshit. Sometimes that's true, but a lot of times it's not. People really are posting their happy moments. They really are having a good life and working hard and enjoying their careers. But happiness in real life still involves a lot of struggle and pain, too. We think these things have to be mutually exclusive—that if you're happy, or you claim to be, it means you have "arrived" and have made it over the threshold that separates happy people from sad people. That you can't be happy while also having a lot of really awful, really horrible moments.

But the truth is that you can be happy and still be in pain at the same time.

I am happy, I am living an incredible life, I am marrying the best person I have ever met. But in addition to all of the beautiful parts that make up these truths, there are also a lot of little ugly pieces, too. I'm still sad a lot, because I'm a human and I have human problems, and my fiancé can help me get through them but he can't make those problems or that sadness go away. I still have terrible anxiety, often related to my physical health. I am terrified to go on trips and to perform in shows and to go places outside of my home, because the whole time I am worried about what I'm going to eat and how I'm going to feel and what I'm going to do if this time the illness will be worse than it's ever been before.

My life is beautiful, joy-filled, full. But it's also ugly, unattractive, embarrassing, painful, bad. You can't have one without the other. Because that's not real.

Too Much Love Is Worse Than None at All

by Sarah Lansky

I have seen the mountains of rural Alaska by biplane and the French Alps from a dock over Lake Geneva. And some mountains in Seattle, Spokane, Vancouver. And some other mountains that I've flown over in planes. I'm nearly certain I've seen the Grand Canyon, or at least a giant crack in the earth somewhere on the left half of the United States. I take pictures of everything I see out airplane windows because I want my husband to see what I see when we aren't together. My seatmates are clearly thinking *are you new,* but I don't care. I wish I was.

I have seen the most beautiful conference rooms in Los Angeles, Cleveland, Saint Louis, New York City, other places. I've seen taxis of all shapes and sizes in every major metropolitan area in the country, and some in Europe, too!

When I sit on my porch and see a plane fly overhead I think to myself *I bet you miss your family, don't you?*

I take lots of aerial pictures of the Coast of Cleveland, as I call it, because I think it's beautiful. People comment things like, "Cleveland is growing on me!" or "looks tropical!" When I check in to my hotel room they ask me if I want a lakeside room, like that's a gift, and I think about how I just saw the lake from the sky and about how the first thing I will do when I get off the elevator and into my room is draw the curtains closed.

I have an ex-boyfriend who only likes my photos when my face looks a certain way. I want to tell him that his life is so much less complicated than he thinks it is—just find a woman with long brown hair and prominent cheekbones. It could be so easy.

One thing I wonder is why do we say that someone "broke" her arm like she did it on purpose? Broke her arm, like she read a book or did her makeup or went to the grocery store.

Everyone who knows me knows I go to the hospital a lot. The explanation is that every part of my body below my neck doesn't work quite right. My digestive system is messed up and I constantly worry that it's my fault. The first time I was hospitalized—while me being hospitalized was still novel—I wouldn't let anyone come to visit. I was worried they would Google my diagnosis and determine that I had done something wrong to invite it. I've now been to the hospital more times than I can count, and nobody asks to visit anymore.

I started an antidepressant and I "browned out" at work two days in a row so I stopped both the antidepressant and trying to go to work, for that week at least. Browning out is like blacking out, except you don't actually lose consciousness. Your eyelids are heavy and you can't follow complex conversation. That sort of thing.

Maybe the parts above my neck don't really work, either!

I was prescribed an antidepressant because I had an appointment with a psychologist at my primary care clinic and I spent about twenty minutes hyperventilating and crying and the last forty she got off her chair and sat on the floor and walked me through breathing exercises because I couldn't speak and all I could talk about was fantasizing about dying, but not really wanting to die in the way that would instigate mandatory reporting. More like dying in my sleep in a fantasy narrative where I'm the central character. Thinking about who would be sent to discover me and what they would think and say. Believing sincerely that I would look sleepy and beautiful, like a delicate and unconscious Disney princess, not at all grotesque and frightening.

In these visions they find me because they send someone out to see why I've not been present, why I've let them down.

In these visions, despite being dead, there is always a smile on my face.

It was enough to earn me a prescription for an anti-depressant. It didn't make me want to die any more or any less. I went to work after that anyway, wiping the mascara stains from under my eyes.

On the way to yet another in a string of endless doctor's appointments, I got lost in the hospital and walked past a lounge area and sat down to try to get my bearings. The man sitting next to me was on the phone with someone, saying over and over, "I failed the alcohol test…I failed it…I don't know what I will do." I didn't even know an "alcohol test" was a thing. He looked so regular. I wanted to hug him for being regular and for being hurt.

Both together at the same time, without combining the two, says my acupuncturist.

I've probably spent more money on Ubers than on car payments in the last eighteen months because driving gives me anxiety. I'm 32 years old and I'm as scared of driving as I was when I was a teen. While driving me home from choir practice in 2001 my mom simply pulled over our minivan, got out, and said I needed to drive home and learn *now* or we were going to stay on that side of the road forever. My mom is not a "tough love" person, but sometimes the truest love is measured.

"Gives me anxiety," as if driving inspires angst on purpose. No psychobiological complicity of my own.

Broad is the road that leads to destruction.

I once went to prison. On a business trip. We went through something like a dozen guarded doors and suddenly found ourselves in the yard with death-row inmates. The sun was shining, the grass was green, and the prisoners were people. Nervous, polite, deferential people in blue jumpsuits with sad smiles and no eye contact. It was bewildering. I was more frightened about the innumerable locked doors I would need to make it through to get back on the outside. And none of them ever would make it outside.

The warden wanted to show us a cell. We went in, looked around, talked about it. Observed the living conditions, the size of the space, the personal effects, made thoughtful comments, nodded. The cell had a little welcome mat that said *Saint Louis Cardinals,* which I can only imagine was a gift or a hard-earned reward, a point of pride, and as the group of us were walking out of the cell someone kicked it accidentally and it got all bunched-up and I stepped over it and walked out behind the group. We invaded someone's home like shame voyeurs, and the least I could've done was to straighten out the rug. For the rest of my life I will wish I had straightened out that rug.

The way the world seems to work is that some people will fool you, and some will want to be fooled. Some are constantly poised for a fight, squatting on their haunches with eyes darting, setting up traps and defenses and seductive smokescreens. Others will only feel the fatal blow after it's been delivered, falling to their knees even before they can turn to see their foe.

But for now we see in a mirror, dimly, but one day we will see face to face.

New Year's Eve and Asleep by 11 PM

by Ari Eastman

He was going to Vegas for a 48-hour trip and I was staying home. And by home, I mean my parents' home. I was 22, freshly out of college, and living up to the boomerang millennial cliché. I had home-cooked meals and spent days watching movies and talking about literature with my mother. Honestly, how could I complain?

Except I could. Because my clinical depression was rearing its ugly head again. Over the summer while I was still living in Los Angeles, I ran out of antidepressants. A more rational person would have remedied that or maybe prevented it from happening in the first place. But I was too busy flying high on an extended manic episode, lusting after a man who would never love me back and starting thousands of projects I'd never finish.

The funny thing is that when you stop taking the anti-depressant that's been keeping the fog of depression at bay, it comes back. Actually, that's not funny at all.

Depression came rushing back and this time, she came with a vengeance. There was an extra bite. A snarl. I was suffocating beneath her.

So there I was, depressed and at home and newly seeing a boy I met through Tinder. He was handsome enough and funny enough and frustratingly intelligent. But what we had was never defined, never the kind of relationship I was going to stay up late writing lovesick poetry about. It wasn't much of a relationship at all. Still, he symbolized something I hadn't felt in so long: I was *wanted.*

Depression convinces you of a lot of dark things. And to suddenly feel wanted, to have someone hunger for me and my body again? Well, I was high off it. I was high off whatever the hell I had with him.

There were nights I questioned if I even liked him or if I had just been drowning in emptiness for so long that this superficial spark was better than nothing. I decided I didn't care.

It was soon going to be New Year's Eve and I had a blue-eyed boy I could escape to. We hadn't been seeing each other long, but I'll admit I felt a little better about myself knowing that this time, THIS New Year's Eve, I was getting that midnight kiss. I couldn't remember the last time I had one. It had been a spell of loneliness and disinterest for so long. Or worse, being hung up on men with girlfriends or men who lived in different time zones.

But I got ahead of myself. That's all that relationship was, really. Getting ahead of myself and the truth and what was actually going on. Trying to hide and hoping I could do it forever. Running away from my problems. Running into a new one.

I found out he was going to Vegas for New Year's Eve and I wasn't going with him. It was a trip he'd planned with his friends long before we met and when my perfectly crafted poker face fell, he feebly tossed a luke-warm invitation. I thanked him but declined. I didn't want to be an afterthought. Especially not in Vegas with a group of people I'd never met.

New Year's Eve came and we texted back and forth, as one does with the guy you're casually sleeping with. He asked what my plans were for the evening. Of course, I lied. I told him I was going to a party or something. The *or something* was supposed to make me detached and cool, you know? Like maybe there was one party! Or two! Who knows?! I'm a woman of mystery and endless opportunities.

I thought about what he'd think if he saw the reality: me, unshowered, sitting in bed at 6 PM. I'd already been able to knock out an entire season of a show. Not entirely unusual for me.

I'd been masquerading as the girl you could hook up with, who would encourage you to go to Vegas without her and not text you back for hours at a time. At the time, my social media was littered with photos of me in bandage dresses and full teeth laughing.

It looked like I went out all the time, a real social butterfly floating in and out of situations without an ounce of anxiety.

I caught a glimpse of myself in my bedroom mirror and felt the fog coming back. This boy, this fling, was a distraction method. I was trying to lose myself in him so depression didn't grab me first. But now, I was alone on New Year's Eve scrolling through Instagram seeing what everyone else was up to. All the things I felt I should have been doing.

He sent me a Snapchat. It was loud and borderline obnoxious, as most Snapchats are. He was in a club of some kind, drunkenly singing with faces I didn't recognize. A girl threw her arm around him and I reminded myself we weren't committed. Still, there was a pang. A sting I couldn't shake.

Two can play that game, I thought, while knowing perfectly well he wasn't playing any sort of game. He was just being 22 and having fun on New Year's Eve.

I jumped in the shower with the water scalding as if it were some test. I tried to see how long I could stand the heat without shrieking. I found a vampy dress hiding in the back of my closet and threw it on. My ass was looking great. And he, along with anyone else following me on Instagram, was going to know it. I applied thick cat eyeliner and the reddest lipstick I had at my disposal.

My mom and stepfather were getting ready to go out (yes, even my parents had plans!). I quickly asked my mom if she could take a few photos of me. She groaned. This is a request I make of her too often. But she agreed.

I held a clutch in my hand, giving it the appearance that I was about to leave for the nightlife any second. I sucked in my stomach. I stuck out my chest. I popped one hip. I analyzed each photo, every insignificant detail. I deleted most of them. This left me with three. The first one was a clear display of my body, angles and curves doing most of the work. The second was a bit more demure, kittenish. I decided on the third, it striking the right balance of *look at my tits* and *I probably have a lot of friends*.

I slapped a filter on, one that slightly offset how pale I was. I mean, I was still pale! But *slightly* less pale. And boom, it was posted.

I refreshed constantly. I watched as likes came in, but none of the ones I wanted. Imagine! I was obsessing over a guy I already regularly had sex with to like my Instagram post! It was some weird validation that I was convinced I needed. Some proof to him, and to myself, that I could be a good time. Look at that photo! That's obviously not a girl spending the evening re-watching episodes of *Buffy the Vampire Slayer*. No, that's a girl ready to paint the town red. Clearly.

Fifteen minutes later, the notification I was desperate for arrived. He double-tapped my li'l heart. A text soon followed.

"You look really hot. Where ya headed?"

I sighed and let my body soak back into bed. I ran a makeup-remover towelette all over my face. I exchanged my dress for an oversized T-shirt once belonging to my late father. I turned my attention back to my laptop. I put my phone underneath my pillow. *I'll get back to him later.*

I was asleep by 11 PM.

For one night, I convinced the world I was someone else.

Is a lie still a lie if no one ever knows?

A Brief History of Being the 'Cool Girl'

by Kendra Syrdal

I am 12 years old.

Slightly older than most of my friends in school due to my September birthday, but still not old enough to say, "Well I'm *older,* so…" to any of them. We're all gathered in Melissa's basement with the lights dimmed, sitting cross-legged in a circle hidden behind some aggressively 70s couch. Her older sister was "watching" us but really, she was too busy going open-legged over her boyfriend to care what her sister and some other middle schoolers were doing at a birthday party.

Had she been paying attention instead of being hormonally 16, she would have found us spinning a bottle of Jones Soda in the middle of the circle. We had two hours until the boys were being sent home—the perfect amount of time to satiate some pre-teen curiosity between the chorus of various Michelle Branch songs and hushed giggles.

Kirsten is explaining to us how to play spin the bottle. She doesn't like me. I never actually figured out why she harbored such an adamant hatred for me, but I do remember it eventually culminating that year in her throwing a can of Diet Coke at my head on the bus. I never rode the bus again.

But that night, in the basement of a house across the street from a cemetery, Kirsten was challenging me in another way.

"You spin this pop bottle," she explained, nonchalantly tossing her flat-ironed blonde hair over her shoulder. "And then whatever boy it lands on you have to kiss."

She locked eyes with me.

"Kendra. You go first."

It was less of a suggestion and more of a challenge in the form of an extended berry lemonade Jones Soda bottle.

And in that moment, my 12-year-old self had a choice.

I could either waver, show my cards that my heart was pounding and I hadn't kissed a boy since I was seven and thought it was funny. Or I could shake my strawberry blonde hair equally as ambivalently, put my shoulders back and my head high, and fake some confidence.

Fake that I didn't care.

Fake that I was a "cool girl."

And I chose the latter.

I yanked that soda bottle out of her hand, spun it around with a little too much force, and planted my lips awkwardly and with as much gusto as I could muster up on Cody's lips from across the circle. We knocked teeth. We didn't make eye contact for the rest of the two hours at the house until Melissa's parents bellowed down the stairs that it was time for the boys to leave.

We never acknowledged that he was my first kiss.

Because cool girls? Cool girls don't have a definable first kiss. Because first kisses don't matter to cool girls. They're *whatever*. They're insignificant.

It later became painfully apparent that Kirsten had a massive crush on Cody and was super-pissed that the Jones Soda bottle hadn't played out in her favor.

Maybe that's why she threw the Diet Coke can.

· · · · · · ·

I'm 14 years old.

I'm shopping with my mother in a T.J. Maxx and I am wildly hungover.

The night before I had been at a sleepover with Sarah who had snuck a bottle of rum from Mexico into the guest room where we were obsessively ranking the boys of our show choir by attractiveness. The rum tasted like suntan lotion. We pulled directly from the bottle and chased with cans of soda, each of us shuddering but pretending like we didn't mind the aggressive taste at *all*.

I never found out if her dad noticed that the bottle with the parrot top went missing from the things he brought back from vacation.

I can feel the rum navigating its way back up my esophagus in the aisle stocked with duvet covers and sham sets. I crouch down, refusing to give in to how disgustingly dehydrated I am. I put my head between my knees, forcing the rum back down where it belongs.

Cool girls aren't weak. They don't give in to hangovers.

So when my mom asks if I want to try on new jeans at The Gap, I say of course. I hyperventilate in the dressing room and chew endless amounts of gum to hopefully hide the residual alcohol smell that I can still taste on my tongue.

I never admit that I feel like shit.

Because cool girls? **Cool girls accept their fate.** They swallow another shot even when they don't particularly want it because they *can*. And it's all about proving that you can. Because can = cool.

So I chug a bottle of Dasani and I continue to pretend that everything's fine.

········

I'm 17 years old.

And I start to fall for an older boy.

We met at a party where I was really drunk and he was stone-cold sober. I was convinced that he was more enamored with Caitlin. Because with her giant eyes and famously red curly hair and long legs, it always seemed like she was the one who got the most attention. We both agreed he was gorgeous and that one of us would like to "add him to our list." We both assumed that if it ever happened in a hypothetical future, it would be her.

But then some months later we ran into each other again. While I was walking around the perimeter of another house party smoking a Camel No. 9 and trying to calm the fuck down, Collin walked with me. Collin made me feel safe.

It was summer. And it was hot. And a cop car drove lazily past us and waved.

We walked a few blocks away from the house where people were shotgunning in the backyard and holing up the bathroom with their cups of UV Blue and Lemonade to gossip down a quiet street. For the first time in months, my heart rate was slowing down. I felt calm. I felt like I could breathe.

We laid in the parking lot of a Lutheran church, shoulder to shoulder, staring up at the sky and listening to the nothingness.

He told me he'd thought about kissing me at that first party but that I was worth waiting for. I told him that I didn't remember the last person I kissed and actually liked it.

He didn't kiss me in that parking lot.

But when he did kiss me, later in his bedroom below the Nietzsche quote on the wall, his lips woke me up. And he told me I had perfect shoulders while he kissed them, too. And he made me feel beautiful.

But I never told Caitlin about it.

Because cool girls don't fall in love.

They bottle everything up. They're beyond emotions and feelings and things that belong between the pages of John Green novels. They don't lay in the parking lots of Lutheran churches talking about heartbreak and abandonment and how they feel like they spin out of control. They hook up and fuck on the pavement and they don't talk about heartbreak because it never happens to them.

Cool girls don't give a shit if they have perfect shoulders or not.

•••••••

I am 18 years old.

Everything is spinning and I'm perched on the bed of the bed of the 1136 house, smoking a cigarette and trying to focus my vision. I don't know how much I drank and can't remember if I ate that day. There are Christmas lights strung above the bed even though it's almost February.

Collin is pacing beside me. He's worried. He wants me to sober up. He wants me to stop panicking.

He tells me, over and over and over, that he wants me to be okay.

And in the middle of trying to get me to stop panicking, the panic overwhelms him. He starts muttering about his roommates and I can see the anger bubbling up inside of him. And so the tables turn, and I want him to be okay.

So I do the only thing I know to get him to stop acting like the world is going to end.

I pull him on top of me, and I strip off my shirt, and I tell him to stop talking for once.

Because I'm a "cool girl."

And cool girls let their bodies do the talking.

So when he goes down on me and tells me he wants me to cum (something that has never happened before), I act like I'm a pro. I don't tell him how foreign it feels to have someone actually care what I'm feeling, care that I enjoy myself during sex. I don't tell him I'm not sure I know *how* to orgasm with another person. I don't tell him thank you for getting me there and showing me how.

And so when after we have sex for the first time, and I drive home with my best friend in the blizzard, and Collin stops talking to me altogether, I don't say anything about that, either.

I don't say anything when he gets a girlfriend more age-appropriate, who's taller, and more self-assured, and looks like a Nasty Gal model. I don't say anything when I hear him call me a "child." I don't say anything when he doesn't even say goodbye when he hears I'm moving away.

Because cool girls? **Cool girls don't care.** They don't need to say anything to anyone.

Because cool girls don't miss people.

·······

I am 19 years old.

My high school ex-boyfriend tells me that it's just fun "for now" when we hook up all of winter break. He calls me the wrong name in bed. He never gets me off. He stops texting me the second I leave the city to go back to college.

I never call him out on it. I never call him on his shit. I let him walk all over me and I pretend that I don't care.

Because I'm a cool girl.

And cool girls definitely don't Facebook-stalk their exes at 2 AM in their dorm rooms while crying to Ingrid Michaelson on repeat.

·······

I'm 20.

I'm in a long-distance relationship. It's putting more that literal miles between us and I can feel myself pulling away.

So when one of my guy friends comes to my bar and pays attention to me, I flirt back.

I buy him a pour of Johnny Walker Blue and entertain the notion that I might have feelings for him, too, even though deep down I know that I'm just lonely. It's not nice. And it's not fair to my boyfriend, who is 436 miles away and my friend who has liked me for years, but I do it anyway.

And any semblance of guilt I feel, I brush to the side. This is just two friends catching up over expensive whiskey. If he reads into it, that's on him. I tell myself anything and everything, taking away whatever responsibility could potentially fall my way.

Cool girls have guy friends, I assure myself. And sometimes those guy friends catch feelings. It's not her fault.

And I never even worry about whether or not it makes me just a cool girl or a cheater or selfish or all of the above when he tries to kiss me after more drinks fall his way. I never tell my boyfriend. I never tell anyone.

Because cool girls have secrets and that's just the way it is.

·······

I'm 23.

I have suspicions that my boyfriend, the one I'm convinced is my person, is cheating on me. I see a Facebook photo of a girl sitting on his lap at a party I didn't attend, looking at him the way I did two years prior when we started dating. I feel those nerves start to tangle up like snakes in the pit of my stomach—my gut telling me that something is up.

I chalk it up to jealousy, to weirdness, to just *really* loving him.

And I never confront him.

Because I'm the cool girlfriend.

I'm the chill girlfriend. The one who never worries about not hearing from him and gives him that Woody Allen/Mia Farrow "waving from across the park" separate togetherness that he previously thought was unobtainable.

I'm the carefree girlfriend. The one who doesn't care that he stays out past 2 AM and doesn't tell me where he's been when he comes home smelling like cigarette smoke and cheap beer.

I'm the cool girlfriend. Who is one of the guys but still owns garter belts and never refuses to go down on him and drinks beer and eats pizza but like Amy Dunn says, still remains a size 2.

Who feels that "oh shit" moment where she realizes he's probably going behind her back, and ignores it.

So I maintain my role as the cool girlfriend.

And when he leaves me for that girl in the photo that was deleted from Facebook, I look in the mirror at my reflection and say,

"I told you so."

· · · · · · ·

I'm 23.

A rebound boyfriend throws me into the wall while we're fighting and calls the cops on me even though he's wasted on God knows what and I'm sober.

I take him back the next day and say I get it, he was drunk. Shit happens. We've all been there.

He tells me how cool I am.

·······

I'm 23.

The same rebound boyfriend asks me to help him put a deposit down on an apartment. He'll pay me back. He promises.

I tell him not to worry about it. Even when months go by and he's still bleeding me dry. I never bring it up.

He thanks me for being so cool.

·······

I'm 24.

I finally leave the shitty relationships behind me and decide to pick up everything and move eight hours away from my college town.

I make it sound like this is my grand plan. That it's my *Wild*. That it's my great escape and that I'll blossom away from my problems into a new version of me that isn't heartbroken or traumatized or scared.

I don't mention that I can't afford it and that my first four months in Seattle are spent alone in a dark room, crying over $3 wine that I bought with found quarters and dimes, terrified that I've made the biggest mistake of my life.

My best friend texts me after I Instagram a photo of my roommate and me in a photo booth on a night where I overdrafted my account in order to buy drinks.

"God your life looks so cool."

•••••••

I'm 26.

I fly over 700 miles to meet Chase because I feel a spark between us and I'm convinced that I am the kind of girl who can take a spontaneous trip to hang out with friends and hook up and not care about it or give it a second thought when it's over.

You know, a cool girl.

And after we do whatever adults do in beds in San Francisco after confusing holidays while drinking Cabernet and Maker's Mark and talking about every-thing from our childhoods to politics, he stops talking to me.

Gone. Nothing. No contact.

Just nothing.

And I act like it doesn't sting. Not even the tiniest bit.

But…it *does*.

It bothers me.

It bothers me that he's gone from talking to me all day every day, to nothing. I didn't ask him to fall in love with me. I didn't ask him to remember my birthday or how I take my coffee or what my dog's name is. I just thought we were friends.

I just expected him to be, well.

I expected him to be just as cool about things as I was being.

But he wasn't.

And that's when I realize something.

Being cool is exhausting. Being cool is unrealistic.

Being cool is grossly overrated.

So even though it means losing all of my cool points, I text him.

"Hey. Question for you. And no pressure if you don't feel like answering so feel free to ignore this. But why did you stop talking to me out of the blue?"

And he gives me some sort of stupid answer and then tries to sext with me again.

But in that moment of watching him flounder while maintaining my chill, my levelness, my "cool," I have a thought.

Maybe there is no such thing as a "cool girl."

Maybe the only thing that matters is being cool with yourself.

Even in those moments that some people would deem deeply uncool.

....

I'm 27.

I'm chatting with my favorite bartender Alex about his best friend Elanor. She's the quintessential girl whom I aesthetically wish I could be. Fair and coiffed with tortoiseshell glasses and impeccable style—she looks like she walked straight out of a Kinfolk edition.

"Alex, she's just one of those intimidatingly cool girls," I say between sips of beer.

He sort of laughs and shakes his head about me.

"I bet a ton of people say that about you."

And I go back to my MacBook with a shrug and a scoff.

Because finally, I don't really care if they say that anymore.

My Daughter, Who Doesn't Want to Be a Mother

by Sarah Bregel

When my daughter Piper was two, she decided she wanted to become a ballerina. My husband and I thought it was too young to start in on the stereotypical "girl" ventures, so we told her that lessons would have to wait. But my child, who is blonde and petite, is also determined. She came out that way, always knowing exactly what she wanted out of life. Saying "not yet" to ballet was my first lesson in arguing with her.

Finally, after a year or so of unwavering dedication to her interest, she wore us down and we signed her up for a class. At seven, she performs in multiple shows a year and even had a leading role in one. I learned never to stand in her way or even try to redirect her. She was already pretty good at directing herself and making her own choices.

Recently, in casual conversation, she demonstrated her strong convictions again. "I don't think I want to be a mommy," she shrugged while coloring at the kitchen table. I paused while loading the dishwasher and stared straight ahead. For a minute, it shocked me. My child was drawn to most other female stereotypes: ballet, dolls, princesses. But motherhood wasn't appealing. I had a few guesses, but I wanted to know why.

I focused my eyes forward and kept on loading, trying to hide my fascination with what she had said. "Oh, yeah? Why's that?" I asked casually. "Because it's hard!" she belted out. "And babies cry like all the time." My first inclination was to blame myself. She'd certainly seen me melt down more than a handful of times, especially during the year after her three-year-old brother was born. Once, after weeks of sleepless nights and not being able to put him down for a minute, I crawled into her bed and let myself cry while she stroked my hair and told me everything would be okay. She was only four years old.

I know a lot of parents who would be devastated to hear that their own child didn't want children. And of course my daughter's mind might change from one week to the next. It certainly may change in the next twenty or so years. But it got me thinking about how we push this idea that motherhood is wonderful and desirable and necessary. We even push it onto our children, even if we ourselves don't believe that's true.

The truth is much grainier. There are aspects of motherhood that are wonderful, yes. But it's every bit as hard as it is good. It is as consuming as it is long. And rarely does it make unhappy people happy. Motherhood, aside from in fleeting moments of bliss, isn't all that dreamy. And while I might fake a smile for the rest of the world, I feel lucky to have a child who really knows me, even (especially) the imperfect parts.

The more I thought about it, her approach to motherhood didn't concern me. It actually seemed smart. Motherhood is the hardest thing I've ever done (or plan to do), and I haven't lied to my daughter about that fact. I haven't lied to my daughter about what it truly means to parent. In fact, I couldn't if I tried. She's in this life with me and she knows what goes on, every minute of it. My perceptive seven-year-old knows that raising kids can be incredible, but it can also be incredibly brutal. I'm okay with that.

The truth is that I have friends in their thirties who know far less about the realities of family life. They're long removed from their childhoods in many ways, or they imagine parenthood will be easier for them than it was for their own parents. If we all didn't share this delusion a little bit, how many of us would actually become parents? Instead, they have a fantasy which comes largely from the mothers on the inside. It comes from our carefully crafted social media posts and lying through our teeth. No—we don't let one another into our four walls often.

At this point in her life, my daughter has a unique perspective, though. She knows how hard raising babies is because she's watched me fall apart a million times and put myself back together. She sees the piles upon piles of laundry that I have to refold when my toddler son knocks them down. She's watched me scrub bodily fluids off nearly every available surface of our home. She lays quietly waiting for me night after night while I spend an hour, sometimes two, getting her brother to sleep so that I can come read with her. She knows that family is my whole world and rarely do I have time for other things. She also knows I struggle with that reality from time to time because I've shared that with her, too. Even if the whole world sees something different, my daughter knows our family is beautiful, but overwhelmingly imperfect.

The conversation soon shifted from why she didn't want to be a mother to all the things she wanted to do with her life. I finished with the dishes and sat down next to her before making dinner. I picked up a blue crayon and colored a heart on the corner of her pictures of fashion drawings—complete outfits with gowns, hats, and shoes. She went on, talking about the different things she wanted to do with her life: dancing, acting, designing dresses. Her list of artistic ventures went on and on, and by the end of the conversation, I felt more pleased with the things she wanted to do than the one thing she said she didn't.

One day when she's grown, she might not remember her own mother's struggles. She might only see the pictures we took on beach vacations and her pretty little baby book—the things we saved because we wanted to. When she's 20 or 30 years removed from this life, she might not remember all the hard things. They might be replaced by images of perfection all around her. She, too, might believe that perfect, blissful motherhood is attainable. I won't remind her how hard it all is. But I also won't push her to have children of her own, either, even if I'm old and gray and yearning for grandbabies. Motherhood is not for everyone, no matter how hard we try to make it look that way.

"That all sounds great," I told her when she was finished reeling off her hopes and dreams. "Ya know, nobody has to be a mother who doesn't want to." She half rolled her eyes and looked at me from a harsh angle, pausing from her drawing. "Everybody knows that, mom," she declared, exasperated. I didn't bother telling her that I don't think everyone actually does know that. That motherhood is the societal norm which most women follow, whether it's truly in their heart to parent or not. I just patted her head and said, "Oh, good!"

Mushy British Face

by Katie Sisneros

I took this picture because the lighting gave my face angles it doesn't actually have.

I was once told I have a "mushy British face" by a man I was sleeping with. I didn't get mad or tell him that's not the sort of thing a person wants to hear. I laughed and said, "Yeah, you're probably right," because my self-esteem is permanently trapped in high school, even though I'm an infinitely more tolerable person than I was then, and probably at least a little better looking. I didn't want to appear unchill or like I cared that much about my appearance, because acting like I don't care is the only way I know how to translate the fact that I don't know *how* to care. I don't know how to improve upon myself.

I don't take a lot of selfies. Many times I've tried, and more than once I've ended up crying on my bedroom floor, exhausted by the knowledge that this is my face, and there's nothing I can do about it. All attempts are immediately deleted, even the ones I kind of like.

I liked this one, though. The lights were shining up on my face in the back room of a small theater at which I was about to perform.

Wide eyes, it hides the fact that one of them droops a little.

Don't smile, your face is getting chubby and smiling just stretches it out like warm Silly Putty.

The lights create cheekbones, a jawline, a chin you don't have.

I was asked by a local online magazine to write something for a live show they were doing. Performing my own writing? Hell, sign me up! My bread and butter! Three decades of hyperactivity, and overactive imagination, and a broken "down" volume button had finally, mercifully, been honed into something vaguely resembling talent. The trick, I learned, is to insist strongly to yourself that you don't give a flying shit what anybody thinks of you, even though you know that really super isn't true. That lie is usually strong enough to get me through stage time and is indistinguishable from confidence to the outside observer. Unlike selfies, this was a world I knew how to navigate.

One of the organizers of this event was a man I didn't know very well but had always thought was extremely handsome whenever we'd end up at the same social events. "The second most handsome man in the Twin Cities," I jokingly called him to myself, and to him whenever I'd had just enough alcohol at one of those social events to hide the fact that he intimidated the crap out of me. Everything went well, I felt confident dorking out into a microphone in front of a hundred or so people, I wore heels not because I thought they would make me look good—I walk like a drunk newborn giraffe in heels—but because I knew they'd force me to stand in one spot with upright posture.

Handsome man and I would eventually spend a night with each other, and some more nights after that, definitely prompted less by the fact that he was interested in seeing me regularly and more by the fact that our first night together ended his long-term relationship the next morning.

His life was falling apart and I wanted desperately to believe he wanted to be around me for reasons other than he suddenly found himself kicked out of his own apartment. He broke down and drank and wore his pain like the gold-plated epaulets of a high-ranking soldier, a tortured artist gracing the world with the wisdom of his introspection. I smiled and drank and sucked in my gut and was always extremely conscious of the angle of depth between my chin and my neck.

Having somehow managed to spend a lot of time with men who think they're cooler/funnier/better/ more attractive than me has planted what sometimes feels like a tiny but extremely dense black stone in the middle of my heart. Sometimes it sprouts like a seed, and thorny tendrils wrap themselves around my throat from the inside and I cannot find a way to speak for myself.

An ex-boyfriend who commented on the fact that I don't wear fashionable jeans.

A sometimes hook-up who wanted a long-winded explanation of what I liked most about the thing he wrote that he'd just read me, but who thinks my writing is just "pretty good."

A new man I started seeing who ended it suddenly after telling me I'm too "normal" and "kind of boring."

I cannot escape the fear that men in my life are just waiting for the right moment to explain something delicate to me. "Katie, I don't really know how to tell you this, so I'll just come out and say it: You're not actually that funny." "Don't take this the wrong way, Katie, but your eyes are kind of lopsided." And they'd all of course be right, these are things I've known all along, thank you for your honesty, and sometimes the anxiety of sitting around waiting for someone to finally give it to me straight is enough to keep me in bed forever. If I don't leave the house, they won't see me do or say or look like something that they don't like.

I took this picture because the woman in it isn't me. Or rather, more precisely, she's the sometimes me I wish I could be all the time. She's a woman that, in response to a man telling her she has a mushy British face, would say, "You're fuckin' right I do!" and then punch him square in the jaw. She's a woman that wouldn't let a man emotionally monopolize their conversation just because he's good-looking and she figures she has to submit in order to keep him around. She's a woman that knows beyond a shadow of a doubt that of all the things she is or might be, normal and boring definitely aren't among them.

Tell Me I'm Funny

by Katie Mather

I'm a very private person, which makes writing for the Internet sort of weird. Weirder than it already is to write for the Internet. Like, the Internet is a super fucking weird place and a lot of the time it makes me want to cry—but I want to write and be good at it and when you feel that strongly about accomplishing either, you go to the Internet.

I actively try to make my entire online presence funny. Admitting this is devastating to me because I feel like when I say something as confident as, "I write funny articles!" then I should be *a lot* funnier in person or something.

The reality is I try very, very hard to come off a specific way—a very chic and aloof 20-something woman who has no time for feelings, dammit!—online. To some degree, my Internet presence is very much an extension of who I genuinely am in person, although it's always a *deliberate* and *controlled* extension. Sure, here are some feelings I've really felt, here are some experiences I've actually had, here are some streams of consciousness inspired by texts I sent myself at

2:48 AM. The Internet thinks it knows me from all of this—even people in my life think they know me better from all of this—but the Internet will always see me how I want it to see me.

And so far, it's worked. I've gotten messages from women telling me that the shrill inner narrative I've published about waiting two hours for someone to text back was the most relatable thing they've ever read; and I've received messages from men telling me to close my whore legs and stop making fun of people named Rob. They're all falling for it! It's amazing!

I'm not exactly sure when I decided what voice I was going to try to embody, but once I figured it out, it felt comfortable and safe and warm. It was this second skin that I could slip into that would protect me from revealing my Actual Self and my Actual Feelings online and in real life.

The second skin made me appear like I wasn't drowning. And if there were any holes and I let it slip that everything was very, very wrong, at least those accidental admissions were dripping in sarcasm or written so dismissively nobody would actually take me seriously.

I had a friend in college who once told me that if she weren't studying to become a doctor, she'd want to be a Tortured Artist. She said it unironically, as if that were just a term you could search along with "in the San Francisco area" on LinkedIn.

I think to her and the rest of the Mentally Healthy outside world, being someone who does something creative professionally means that you are talented enough to manipulate all your inner turmoil into some beautiful, loving thing. This romanticized idea of being a Tortured Artist and wistfully staring out of the window on a rainy day in a petite cafe as you delicately type away at a story that effortlessly came to you that morning in the shower and your hair is so beautiful and glossy and maybe you're smoking a cigarette and wearing a turtleneck too and, like, boys just love you without you even needing to say a word and you're sad, but like, in a very controlled sense where it doesn't destroy you regularly—that's exactly what my friend thought I was getting at when she linked together that I wanted to be a writer *and also* had crippling, undiagnosed depression that made me feel like dying all the time.

(For the record, my response to her was that if I weren't trying to become a writer, I suppose I'd settle for being a Tortured Doctor. She didn't even laugh and I've never gotten over it.)

I don't like writing about my depression. I was raised by a mother who encouraged open discussions about feelings and crying in public, so naturally I am very tight-lipped and suppress everything until someone sets me off and I lash out at them as part of my residual teenage rebellion.

But the main reason why I'm not entirely honest is because depression makes me a horrible person. I become selfish and isolating—it's a curse for someone like me, who feels happiness being surrounded by other people all the time, to simultaneously treat those people like shit and push them away because of a dopamine deficiency.

I feel unhappy, but I also feel like I don't deserve to feel that way.

So instead, I want to distract everyone and divert their attention to wild, over-the-top, and embellished stories and jokes that are so loud and dramatic and in all-caps with a lot of parenthetical hysteria and ex-clamation points and angry sarcasm so that nobody will notice me in the corner feeling lots of things and being sad. Maybe if I scream my jokes loudly enough, I will forget to address all of my feelings, too.

A guy once told me that what he liked about me (LOL) was how laid back I was and how it was nice that I didn't care about things, and I almost exploded because I could not believe my charade was actually working. My second skin. But because he was a Real Life Friend and not some stranger on the Internet, I had to be like, "Oh my god, I have some *terrible news* for you."

I feel like I'm cheating or lying sometimes. Coworkers and I have discussed in great length how unique it is that part of our job is essentially emotionally mastur-bating for a bunch of strangers on the Internet. Being very open and vulnerable and honest on the Internet is *sexy*. And I feel like I'm faking it. I feel a bizarre sense of pressure to be validated by people I don't know and people I will never meet. Tell me I'm funny. Tell me my second skin is working. Tell me you can't even tell how unhappy I am. Tell I'm good at what I do.

I get a lot of varying reactions when I tell people I primarily write for a living, and one time an Uber driver in LA responded to me with:

"To be a good writer, you really have to live, don't you?"

I nearly shoved my body out of the moving vehicle. Is anyone else aware of how hard it is to live sometimes? And how hard it is to talk about it? *Why can't I just keep on pretending to live in my second skin?*

What if my sense of humor only exists because I'm sad? I've seriously considered whether taking care of myself could possibly inhibit me from fulfilling my potential as a writer. What a fucking *bummer* that would be. Why do I have to choose? I don't want to be anyone's tortured-artist fantasy. I honestly just want to be good at writing and be happy. Why does that sound so straightforward but impossible to achieve sometimes?

It took me forever to realize that I had always assumed writing would help me become a Regular Person. I wanted writing to be my fix. I wanted it to make me a better friend, sister, daughter, human being, whatever. I wanted to become a writer and to be content with myself, and I assumed that those two things were a package deal.

Writing does not save me. Living with something like depression is only tolerable when you accept that you will not be fixed. You live with it. I am living with it. But in the meantime, you will only see me in my second skin.

I think it's incredible Regular People can wake up and not feel this way—this frustration, this sadness, this *emptiness*, this necessity to have a second skin in the first place. I forget that living without mental illness is a real thing that real people experience. And here I am, just pretending that I'm one of them on the Internet.

What Cambodia Didn't Fix

by Dana Bedessem

There is a specific rhythm to the day when you have anxiety.

Every night I go to bed swimming in the anxiety of the decisions I've made that day, last week, a year ago, and ones I haven't even made yet. I fret over the unknown circumstances of next week, next year, or the next 10 years. Really, what I'm worried about is, "Am I doing the *right* thing?"

I have always been a worrier. Do you remember in elementary school when the teacher would share their "how I'll always remember you" speech and grant a title of identity to each kid? I was always "the worrier," or worse, "the worry wart." No 10-year-old girl wants a title with the word "wart" in it.

I had my first nervous breakdown when I was 24. I remember falling to the floor in my bedroom. The room shifted and rolled under my feet. I dropped into a ball and gasped for air. I don't remember crying. I do remember thinking I was crazy.

I went to a hypnotist. She would record each meditation exercise we'd do in our session so I could listen to it whenever I felt panicked. The meditations helped get me through sleepless nights and cycles of questions. I bounced back, but the root of it all stayed inside me somewhere hibernating.

I used to drive up and down the hilly streets of San Francisco with one hand over my chest willing myself not to look at the garages underneath the ominous Victorians. Someone had told me homes with garages were unstable—the worst place to be in an earthquake. I thought about the families living inside and the false sense of security a big beautiful home like that must provide them. Didn't they know? Earthquakes are unpredictable.

The second breakdown happened years later when I was 27. It wasn't a one-moment snap like the first. It was a slow, steady trickle of anxiety. I had a beautiful apartment in Pacific Heights. From my living-room window I saw the blanket of expensive homes rolling across the city, all the way up to Sutro Tower. I had a good job. A great boyfriend. I'd never been so unhappy.

My emotions were unmanageable. I fought back by developing habits that put me in control. I ran every morning with a friend by the water. When running, I avoided all the cracks in the sidewalk. My calves were insane that year.

I eventually quit my job. I didn't work for six months. I traveled a lot. I went back home and stayed with my parents for three weeks. I went to Cambodia and Vietnam for four weeks. I tried to "find myself."

I stumbled upon a shaman in Cambodia and spoke with him about my life. It was $200 worth of speaking about my life, to be exact. He told me my dead grandfather loved me. That in one of my past lives I smoked a pipe. In another, I was raped and murdered at around 12 or 14 while traveling west with my family in a covered wagon. In most of my past lives I was a man. He told me I find white men less attractive than men of color. He explained to me how the soul splits when you die and fractions of your soul move into new lives. It's reincarnation, but more importantly, it's the explanation for soul mates. He told me a lot of things: some of them crazy, some of them true, and some I may never know if they are or will be true. He told me that in order to get back on my "path," the universe wanted me to move home. So, I did.

I came home from that trip and moved out of my great San Francisco apartment where I lived with my great boyfriend. With each shirt I folded and knick-knack I wrapped, I took a deep breath and resigned myself to placing each item in a box.

That whole week the air was thick with emotions, but there was one day my boyfriend and I taught each other how to ballroom dance. On that day, we swung between uncontrollable fits of crying to YouTubing "how to waltz." We thought we were giving each other a break from the tears. Looking back, we were discovering how to love and support each other when things weren't predictable because we never had to think about it before.

When I landed in Minneapolis my brother picked me up at the airport. I planned to stay with him and my sister-in-law for three months until I figured out what I was doing. After I got off the plane, I hid in the bathroom for 30 minutes crying and ignoring the string of texts and calls asking where I was.

Eventually, I came out of the bathroom and found my brother.

I've been in Minneapolis for two years. I wish I could say my story of traveling alone, meeting a shaman, and moving to a new city has been rolled up into a package of peace, contentment, and self-confidence. I wish I could say I am completely whole now. I'm still on that journey.

Those experiences weren't for nothing. I'm better. I think. At least, I can level myself in shaky moments.

Like when I go to bed at night and question if I'm doing what I should be doing. If my move, my extracurricular activities, my job, those Oreos I ate, or didn't eat, were the right decisions for me. Wondering if I'm going in the "right direction."

Then I wake up and remind myself there are no earthquakes in Minnesota.

Beach Vacation Blues

by Koty Neelis

I like to consider myself an adventurous person. I've boarded down a volcano going 40 miles per hour in Central America, lived on top of a mountain in a tiny village in France, and backpacked alone through some of the most remote parts of the world. But there is one thing I've done while traveling I will never do again—stay at an all-inclusive resort.

An all-inclusive resort is the worst place to spend Christmas when you're vacationing alone, it turns out. I learned this the hard way when I spent the holiday in Playa del Carmen, Mexico, nearly 3,000 miles away from the dreary concrete winter wonderland of my home in Chicago. It had been a hard year both personally and professionally, and all I wanted was to drink my sadness away at the beach and distract myself by going on bike rides, eating copious amounts of Mexican food, and reading in the Caribbean sunshine. Like other trips I've taken by myself I envisioned excitement of the unknown, adventure, and the chance to make new friends along the way.

I wanted to detox from all the negativity I had experienced over the past year and reset myself both mentally and physically, just in time for the new year.

For the first time in my life I was making enough money to not only pay my bills, but to save money *and* upgrade little things in my life I had been putting off for forever, like buying new bedding and dishes that actually match. *Did I also want to upgrade the way I traveled?* I asked myself on a snowy night at 3 AM while browsing some resort website half-asleep. With descriptions like "upscale," "gourmet dining experience," "magnificent white sand beaches with azure waters," and "ultimate rest and rejuvenation," I was sold. I wasn't sure if I had ever experienced any of those things before, but my bank account (and my exhausted, pale body) screamed at me, "You deserve this!! You've worked so hard this year!! Live your best life!"

So I did it. I booked my vacation at an all-inclusive resort and I felt very grown-up about the whole thing. This is how *adults* traveled. No longer would I share a bunk bed in a dorm room with a group of other travelers stumbling in through all hours of the night. I'd have my own room and a luxurious bed to fall asleep in while listening to the ocean waves crash against the beach. I'd dine at the incredible restaurants listed on the resort's website and have "delicious international cuisine crafted by the finest chefs in the region." I'd get a tan, do yoga, and drink piña coladas on the beach with my impossibly interesting new resort friends. I'd head back to Chicago after a week on the beach an improved version of myself ready to kick 2017's ass.

Yeah, no. None of that happened.

It rained nearly the entire time I was there. And not just a little light rain here and there; it was like monsoon-style downpours almost every day, except for a few cloudless, rain-free moments I took advantage of to show off on social media. The ocean view I was promised when I booked my room? They should have called it "bar view," because that's all I could see from my room. The actual ocean-view rooms were for "diamond members." The food at the resort was mediocre at best and not much different than what you'd find at a local TGI Fridays. All the fun daily activities on the resort they advertised? Really only doable if you have a partner. And *everyone* at the resort had a partner. Except me. Everywhere I looked I was reminded of just how alone I was. Between not being able to participate in resort events and being gawked at by people when I dined alone (granted, one night I *did* bring 10 tiny desserts back to my table from the buffet, which probably looked funny, but I regret nothing), everywhere I went I was reminded of my aloneness. All my cool new friends I thought I'd make? It turns out couples don't really like single women hanging out around them!

Now, I like to think that I'm the kind of person that can talk to anyone. As a writer I've always taken pride in being able to get anyone to open up and tell me their stories, especially while traveling. I've had some amazing, life-changing conversations with people I had only met a couple of hours before, and I was determined to have a similar experience on this trip as well.

One afternoon around 2 PM I heard Justin Bieber's "Sorry" come on over the speakers at the bar next to my room just as the rain was beginning to let up a little. I had spent the morning lying in bed feeling despondent about the way the trip was going, but hearing one of my favorite songs perked me up. I saw some people had gathered around the bar and I thought, "Maybe I'm just being hypersensitive. I've always traveled alone and made friends with strangers regardless of where I was. Maybe I'm just in a funky mindset and need to pull myself out of it." I put on some sunblock, threw on a cute sundress I hoped would make me seem approachable instead of threatening, and grabbed my sunglasses in hopes the sun would actually appear that day.

I snatched a seat at the bar next to a couple with dark, leathery tans, gold jewelry, and bleached-blonde hair. After taking a sip from my gin and tonic I turned to my left and cold-opened a woman wearing a leopard-print visor with the only thing I could really think of saying. "Man, this weather really sucks, huh?"

"Yeah, no shit, honey," she replied with a smile. She turned to her husband and whispered something, prompting him to grab their drinks and wander away. Damn, okay. Clearly, we were not going to be having any life-changing conversations today.

Despite trying to be friendly toward others I saw around the resort, I spent the rest of the trip in almost complete silence. Even if my Instagram and Facebook showed pictures of blue skies and envy-inducing afternoons on the beach to all of my friends suffering the cold winter in Chicago, I wasn't any happier.

On Christmas Day it rained heavily in the morning, but the skies opened up in the afternoon. I posted a photo to Instagram of an idyllic setting of me holding a piña colada while relaxing next to the ocean. To my friends and family I was cool and independent for doing something untraditional for the holidays, and they agreed that after having a hell of a year, I totally deserved this. While sitting there on the beach I thought about how I had so many things to celebrate and appreciate. I'd just received a raise, a promotion, and an end-of-year bonus at work before I left for my trip. I had reached several milestones recently that even five years ago would have seemed impossible. Why, then, did I still feel so alone?

I messaged my boyfriend, who was spending the holiday with his family in Kansas and told him I missed him and wished we could be together. I was looking for some kind of human connection, something to curb my loneliness after a week of unintended isolation. He had spent the past year dealing with a lot of heavy mental-health issues and I had been supportive and encouraging the whole way. He was never one to openly express his emotions, and I'm not entirely sure why I thought anything had changed, but it was Christmas and I was thousands of miles away, so I thought maybe I'd get an "I miss you, too!" or "I can't wait to see you" back. It never came. I realized the emotional dissonance between us was so strong, it felt like a glaring red flag of how ignorant my optimism could really be. And from there my loneliness spiraled from the depths of my chest down into my stomach until the feeling was so heavy and profound I felt like I could reach right in and grab it.

Looking around at the other couples surrounding me on the beach I wondered why I had taken this trip at all, if I really could have been so naive to think an expensive vacation would make me feel better. And even worse, I questioned if I'd ever even be in the kind of relationship where two people happily make plans and travel together and spend their Christmases by each other's side. I had worked hard to reach a lot of milestones, and I was proud of my accomplishments, but the one thing I still couldn't figure out was how to navigate dating and relationships—the one thing that seems to come so easily to everyone else. Suddenly, I felt like an alien next to all of these happy couples.

On the flight back to Chicago I realized why my trip had ultimately been a huge disappointment. The problem wasn't the bad weather, the bad food at the resort, or even the lack of connection and friendliness from other travelers. The problem was that I had taken this trip with the idea that healing myself could only happen by removing myself from my everyday life and immersing myself in a different environment and an experience I could pay for. I had spent the entire week in Mexico looking for outside stimuli to make me feel complete and less alone, but in reality none of those feelings of wholeness were going to come from anything but myself. It didn't matter how far away I traveled or how many idyllic vacation pictures I took; true fulfillment wasn't going to come in a quick fix or impromptu beach trip.

Perfect Pictures Don't Stop Ugly Thoughts

by Kaitlin Chappell Rogers

The moment the "We're engaged" picture gets posted on Instagram and Facebook, that's when it all starts. For me, it was a whirlwind. The day before that picture was posted, I was homesick with my eyes swollen shut from some weird allergies and was probably crying about the job I wanted to quit. Life was way less than perfect. I had suspicions that my boyfriend would propose the following day because it marked a year since he asked me on our first date. While I was at work the next day, he accidentally sent me the text meant for the photographer he had hired, and I knew my suspicions were correct.

He tried to cover it up, but I knew it was really about to happen; so, I did what any girl would do, right? I went to get my nails done and buy a new outfit! (OK, maybe any girl wouldn't do that, but I did.)

And he did propose. He took me to several different places that meant a lot to us and surprised me with friends and family and a photographer to capture the moment. He and my best friends even threw a surprise engagement party to end the night. It really was a beautiful, perfect disaster, and I loved it.

But after the initial awe wore off, the "We're engaged" picture was posted, and the likes and congratulations texts rolled in, I went to that place of "not good enough."

Is the ring big enough? Did I pick the right one? Maybe I shouldn't have told him I wanted family and a photographer there. Should it have been just us two? Maybe I should have let him come up with everything on his own and do it when and where he wanted. Where will we get married? What dress will I wear? What if our wedding isn't perfect? You see someone else's pictures on Instagram of her road to her happily ever after, but what you don't know is the backstory.

It was out of control.

I had to realize that just because a girl posts an adorable picture of her finding her wedding dress doesn't mean she didn't break down right after she took the picture. Just because someone got engaged in Bali and posted the most breathtaking picture of the most breathtaking view with the most breathtaking ring and the most breathtaking guy does not mean she will have more breathtaking moments than you in this life. She will have hers and you will have yours and none are better or more valuable because they are all different.

The pictures the photographer took were perfect, and everyone on social media and in real life showered us with love. But perfect pictures don't stop the ugly thoughts.

What no one tells you about wedding planning is that you're still just you. The fun of being a bride-to-be does not imbue you with the magical quality of having it all together. I've struggled with comparison for as long as I can remember. I have days when I'm confident in the woman I believe God created me to be, and then I have days when I want to be someone else.

When I got engaged, I never imagined my comparison battle getting worse, because I've never heard anyone talk about that when they talk about wedding planning, but I realized becoming a bride can lead you to compare yourself like never before if you let it.

For me, it has been a long, winding, exciting road, but it has been a stressful one, too, and I let myself become more stressed out by trying to keep up with everyone around me getting married. It seemed like when I got engaged, everyone else either got engaged just before me or right after me. And it's a lot of fun to walk through that season with other people to share ideas and struggles, but comparison can creep in and suck all the fun out of the season if you let it get its foot in the door.

Now, the entire engagement wasn't stressful; don't get me wrong. There were plenty of times when I was totally focused on what mattered—our union and the love we share. I knew we would have a beautiful wedding with all of our favorite people celebrating our incredible, godly love story—my favorite story to tell.

But in between all the perfect moments and Instagram posts with mushy captions were some valleys that I had to climb out of.

Boss Bitch

by Jen Kilgo

This coming fall, I will celebrate four years of living an incredible dream that many people aspire to,
day in and day out, as they drive the same route to
work...in the same car...to the same job: the dream
of breaking free from the "man" and finally working
for oneself.

Working for myself—or being an "entrepreneuress,"
as I like to say—is hands-down one of the best, most
liberating things I've done in my life. I am literally
the boss. I call the shots, y'all. Two-hour lunches with
friends over sushi on a Tuesday? Check. Not working
on Fridays, because, Fridays? Check. Deciding on a
whim to take a trip to Morocco for two weeks? Done.

Gone are the horrible days of "requesting" time off,
agonizing over whether to use another precious vacation day to travel out of state for a friend's wedding.
No longer do I rush out the door in the morning, late
again, sucking down coffee so I can appear relatively
engaged during the most pointless and unproductive
weekly 8 AM Wednesday meeting EVER. And I never,
ever have to put on a fake grin for some egotistical

higher-up who needs to feel important while making others around him feel small. All of this is priceless. I could go on and on about the joys and freedom of taking the leap into this wonderful and exhilarating new world.

Here's the thing, though…my new boss? Lately she's been a total BITCH. So stressed out. Just yesterday she booked me for seven hours back-to-back without a break because she's "anxious about money." She talks *ad nauseam* about the "investors" (read: credit cards) breathing down her neck and how we need to pay them off faster…FASTER! Sometimes she wakes up at 2 AM in a full body sweat because she's terrified that today is the day it's all actually going to fall apart. I try to reason with her, saying, hey, sistafriend! LOOK at what you've done here! You're paying the bills! The business is growing every year, and our clients are happy! They're thriving and they absolutely love coming here. They're sending us their friends, and we're changing the world for the better. Relax!

Some days she can hear me. She can smile and feel proud of herself and clear some space for a yoga class and a massage. I'm so very proud of her when she does this. I can see how much of a difference it makes in her mood, her overall health. But many days over the last few years that I've been working here, I've watched her nearly fall apart under the pressure. I've watched her sleep suffer and her anxiety shoot through the roof. I can tell how much she believes in what she's doing (and she's really good at it!)— but she can't seem to slow down. She's always scared that there won't be enough. That she's totally alone in the world. That our company is not going to make it. That no one will ever show up for her or take care of her if she doesn't do it ALL ten times faster and better than everyone expects.

I joined her last week for her biweekly session at her therapist's office. She wept as I told her that I see how hard she's working and how deeply she cares for people, but that I can't watch her run herself into the ground any longer. I told her that she matters just as much as everyone else…yet she seems to have forgotten. I asked her if she might let me hold her accountable for taking better care of herself, reminding her that if she goes down, the whole fucking ship goes down. I asked her to consider what she's so afraid of that keeps her moving at such a pace.

She sobbed as she told me that she doesn't know how to slow down sometimes, because in the past, the bottom actually DID fall out. In her family. In her life. And she's utterly terrified it will happen again.

I held her hand and told her that her fear makes sense. Then I reminded her that FEAR IS ALWAYS A LIAR. Always. It wants us to believe that we're alone in the world, that there is no God, no universe, nothing of love conspiring for our highest good. It wants to destroy us with whatever it can: busyness, addiction, depression, hopelessness. Fear is always, always a liar. And she knows this. She believes this. She just seems to have forgotten.

As much of a slave-driver as my boss can be sometimes, I know it's because she's scared. We're planning lots of yoga and meditation next week, and she's promised me at least two long lunches with friends. It's a learning curve for sure...but I think I'll stick around here for a while. I feel like we might just be starting to get the hang of how to do this entrepreneuress life.

Hot Lava

by Nikita Gill

People always ask me where I got my claws. They describe my writing as fearless, and I think back to the person I used to be, the person who was scared and always unsure of which move to make. The person who had become a victim and stayed that way for a long time.

Once upon a time in a faraway land lived a version of me that was so intimidated, she didn't know how to speak without someone telling her to speak up. Let's start with an incident that still makes my bones throb with anger.

"Hey! Hey you, sexy!"

I heard these words being yelled across the street in Hindi, and I swallowed hard. My peripheral vision told me there was a group of men standing there, all with the same cheesy grin on their face, melding into one huge, terrifying entity. I clenched my fists and lowered my head. *Just walk, walk and they won't bother you anymore.*

"Hey, what do you think, you're too good for us?"

The rising panic was slowly replaced with fear. This particular road was a relatively busy one, but that didn't matter. There were at least six of them. Even at 3 o'clock in the afternoon in the middle of the streets in New Delhi, if I so much as made eye contact, this could be taken as an invitation to grab me, bundle me into a van, and take me to some unknown location to do hideous things to me.

Please go away, my mind chanted as I began to walk faster, very aware that they were following me now.

Please. Suddenly I felt a hand grab my bag and pull. I was surprised but turned to face my attacker, yanking it back and away from him. My eyes were wide, fearful as I realized that not only had they caught up to me, but they had surrounded me. My attacker, a huge man with a set of white shark teeth, yanked hard enough that my bag almost broke. I almost screamed in fear as I smelled bodies too close to me, my throat closing up. Grasping the strap of my bag as hard as I could, I shoved through the gang and ran as fast as my legs could carry me.

I didn't stop until I knew I had outrun them and I didn't feel safe until I was finally home with my parents. I'd like to say this was an isolated incident, that it was just the one time, that things like this don't happen often in New Delhi, but unfortunately, growing up female in New Delhi also meant growing up scared, growing up being told not to retaliate, that it doesn't matter if their gaze makes you uncomfortable, their comments make you sick to your stomach; you ignore it and you keep walking. Making eye contact, turning around and yelling to protect your dignity, putting them in their place was unacceptable because any of these things can be misconstrued as an invitation. Instead, everyone who loves you teaches you as a woman to ignore it. They teach you that being safe means being scared, not dressing the way you want to, never looking up. Never making eye contact. Never coming home late. Never catching the last train home from anywhere because any of these things can lead to rape.

The undertone of sexual aggression toward women fosters an atmosphere of intimidation, a hunted look in every woman's eye the moment she steps onto the streets, even in the middle of the day, even if it is just to get her groceries. There is a terror there that is hard to explain, and even when you are with your girlfriends, there is always a part of you that is alert in every way.

And I, like most girls, grew up with this fear that I, too, would one day be victimized. That one day a man would just take my body like it is his and—what is worse—people will say that it was my own fault for not ignoring his filthy insults.

We carry every word inside us. Every attempted grope, every man who stands too close, every gaze that undresses us with their eyes. They live inside us like poison, encouraging the fear, the intimidation.

But everything has a boiling point. For some of us, like me, anger began to take the place of everything that was so terrifying. Instead of bile, I felt hot lava caged inside my stomach, dying to come out.

I remember clearly the first time I lashed out at a man who was deliberately standing too close to me. My eyes were not wide with fear, they were now narrow with disgust and anger at his audacity. I remember shaking—not with terror, but with the sheer urge to shove him. And for a change, it wasn't me who was scared. He seemed frightened and fell back against his friends because he thought I was going to slap him silly.

This, this is what it felt like, I had thought in wonder as I watched him scurry away. This is how it feels to have control finally, to say what I feel finally. And although a little part of me still thinks of the retaliation, I refuse to chain the lioness up again now that she is free, the wildest part of me still protecting me.

From being scared, fearful, and intimidated, I learned how to embrace the flames within myself. That was how I learned to take the first steps to fearless, clawing my way out of the abyss called fear, reaching out and finally feeling the sun on my face. I am learning what it is like to stand up for myself. And it is the most liberating feeling ever.

My Social Media Life Is Bullshit (And I Feel Fine)

by Mélanie Berliet

Last night I spent half an hour doctoring photos into an Instagram post that never came to fruition. The goal was to crop a photo of myself hovering above an image of the college students I guest-lectured recently because their professor uses my work as a teaching tool. Pretty cool, right? I felt honored to address a group of young, aspiring journalists and I wanted to humblebrag about it over social. The problem was, I couldn't create a photo collage that made the classroom look sufficiently populated, so I chose to forgo posting about the experience altogether.

Last week I posted a selfie in which I'm holding my dress slightly above my 21-week baby bump. The caption reads "Popped!" plus a few adorable emojis. I posted this photo because I knew it would receive a ton of likes, and I was craving an ego boost at the time. But the truth is that I don't feel good about my pregnant body. Plus, getting that Insta-worthy picture required contorting my face and body into slightly different variations of the same pose while standing in front of a full-length mirror for a crazy amount of time. I probably took 25 photos before narrowing it down to the one that made the cut. And then it took 15 minutes for me to settle on the exact right shade of image brightness and wording for the accompanying caption.

Last month my boyfriend and I had a massive fight. Things got really ugly, as they do every so often between long-term couples. I'm not ashamed that my boyfriend and I fight, but I never hint at our schisms on social. In fact, I tend to post a happy couple photo in the wake of every brawl, including this last one. It's as if I'm finalizing our reconciliation with a smiley, romantic photo (either a recent shot or a throwback pulled expressly for this purpose) by reminding myself (and my followers) that there've been so many good times and there will be more. When I do this, I'm not seeking approval so much as broadcasting relief that the nastiness has subsided—reminding myself that I can still love the man who sometimes drives me absolutely nuts.

·······

I like to think of myself as a truthful person. In my writing, I address a lot of things most people shy away from, like pubic hair, phone sex, recreational drug use, and infidelity. But my social-media presence doesn't reflect the brand of honesty I associate with my writing. Why? Because people don't seem to "like" the truth, at least not from my experience.

Often, people email me sincere notes of appreciation after reading my most brutally honest work. These people typically Google their way to essays I've written about "what it's really like to be in a relationship with your goddamn soul mate," probably because they're in the midst of a lovers' quarrel and my words bring them comfort. They are seeking the truth rather than happening upon it. When I post excerpts from similarly themed articles on my Facebook and Instagram accounts, they reliably tank.

From what I can gather, people don't lean on social media for that sense of solidarity they seek when browsing the Internet for specific answers. Maybe because they know they can't find it there. Or maybe because they don't want to find it there.

When I think about our collective, over-glossed approach to social media, I go back and forth. Part of me hates the girl I am while hesitating for way too many minutes between slightly different Instagram filters before committing fully to the share button. But another part of me doesn't really care that my social presence is ridiculously inauthentic.

I've never understood the argument that magazine publishers and editors should be held accountable for women's body-image issues. The way I see it, magazines are riddled with images of way-too-thin women because whether we like it or not, those images sell magazines. The beauty industry is inherently aspirational, and the people who purchase magazines have historically favored glossies featuring impossibly thin, gorgeous gazelles in place of "real people."

How can you blame the professionals behind a magazine for giving their readers exactly what they want? And how can you blame me or anyone else for giving their followers exactly what they want?

The question of whether to condemn the media or consumers for society's widespread body dysmorphia is a classic chicken-or-egg type problem, one that seems to extend to our over-beautified social feeds.

So what if my social media life looks so much awesomer than my real life? It's curated proactively in response to user feedback. My social presence is designed to appeal to distant spectators. It's intended as entertainment. A means of glimpsing a sliver of my actual existence. It's not a reflection of my inner core, which I will very willingly share upon request with my nearest and dearest, or any of my readers.

Total honestly might work for some on social, but it doesn't work for me, and I'm okay with that. I don't think I'm contributing to some larger societal dilemma. I'm just partaking in a lighthearted game, the same voyeuristic game I expect my former high school and college classmates to partake in. Why? Because it's fun! It's oddly satisfying to peek at someone else's day to day. I just like to remind myself that behind every happy couple hashtag is a real-life argument, behind every spotless forehead is a photo-editing app, and behind every Caribbean sunset is a journey marked by overstuffed suitcases and airport hiccups.

Instead of getting all frazzled about how much our social-media lives deviate from reality, I choose to be mindful as I sift through my feeds. I don't feel responsible for being 100 percent honest with the strangers and acquaintances who choose to follow me, and I don't expect others to, either. Each of us gets to decide how we present ourselves to the social-media world, and if all I want to provide is a tiny dose of half-truth to sate my followers' need for some digital escapism, I think that's just fine.

I Don't Want a Los Angeles Kind of Love

by Chrissy Stockton

I was in LA for work; a friend lived there. She occupied the peculiar space of someone who I called a friend without having ever spent much time talking to them, the person who is in the periphery of your life long enough that you start to mistake continuity for closeness. I was visiting her city and there seemed to be some kind of unspoken obligation to meet up. I remembered her to be somewhat crude and abrasive, but this is the way I think everyone from the Midwest describes everyone from large coastal cities, not some specific moral failing on her part. There are inverse descriptions of the sloppy lethargy or timid, dopey efforts those city dwellers might associate with flyover states.

I walked to a grocery store and bought some waters and a container of pre-cut fruit and we met at a park near my hotel. I love city parks because I like how people are less prissy there than everywhere else, letting their shoes slide off and enjoying the sun and the dirt on their bare skin for a bit. They are places people connect to their bodies, an intentional rarity in the urban world.

She arrived breathless from across town and launched into a life update that I could tell had been rehearsed and repeated many times, a play-acting of a social custom. The "how are you" was perfunctory; she expected me to say "good" or "fine," which was okay with me to start. But I was anxious to drop the pretense. I was on what felt like a vacation and I wanted to have a vacation-type conversation. We were almost strangers; in a way, I wanted to open up the curious way you can with someone you see only between lengthy intervals of not speaking.

But it didn't happen between the two of us, for whatever reason. We lasted about an hour, grasping for anything that felt like a connection, any way to feel like we were speaking the same language for a short time. What I offered felt weak, some soft subjects she wasn't interested in. And I felt embarrassed about the hardness of the conversation, a vulgar litany of the skeletal structure of her outward life. I heard about her job and how much money she makes and the famous people she's met and all the other companies that are offering her jobs. I felt deeply ashamed about her mistaken belief that these were tokens she needed to offer me in exchange for my attention or reverence or affection.

When she left her seat and joined me supine in the grass, I felt a flare of hope. But she handed me her phone and asked me to take some photos of her so she could post one on Instagram. It was strange to try to capture the aesthetic of the afternoon we didn't have: a casual bout of relaxation, dressed down, in close contact with our biological status as animals. We went through several rounds of her instructions and my inept attempts at influencer photography. I wasn't good at getting what she wanted. I was awkward, guilty for the part I was playing in an act so devoid of exactly the human element I was craving. I looked later; she didn't post any of the photos.

After she left I stayed in the park, cross-legged in the grass. I tried to shake the feeling that I had disappointed this girl. I hadn't known how to be a captive enough audience for her fraudulence. I hadn't been able to take a decent picture, the sort of receipt that would have indicated the afternoon had been well spent.

The previous summer a friend I hadn't seen in years and didn't know well to begin with was in my city for a family wedding. We met up and had a drink and exhausted all the things we had to talk about or catch up on over that hour. We walked to a dock at the lake by my apartment and laid on it and enjoyed having our feet in the water and the sun on our faces and eyes closed—listening to the boat sounds and the people sounds and being quiet together. I felt understood in all that silence in an inverse way all the talking with this girl had made me feel alone, like falling asleep on the train and waking up far from where you intended to be, perhaps in a place where your language is no longer spoken.

I don't want to write about how this friend is mean or bad or a worse person than me, because I don't believe that. But that afternoon I was trying to press my soft body up against something hard and rough, industrial but wearing human skin. I became aware that this was a thing, a normal way of being in the world and that I was the odd one, the one who needed it to be something more. The one who couldn't be fed by the standard fare. I became aware of the ways I didn't fit into the exchange of currency people offer themselves as, not here, out of my element. I couldn't provide, I couldn't be provided for.

All Light Contains Dark Things

by Brianna Wiest

Writers write what they know—and in the era of confessional media, our subject is what we know best: ourselves. The result is that a writer's biggest asset is the worst thing that's happened to them. And it's always just that—what *happened* to them. Read almost any personal essay online—and there are a lot—the author will almost always frame their most personal and revealing stories from the perspective of their current selves reflecting on their former. They talk about their traumas in the safety of the past tense. The moral of the story is why they're better *now* and why you should adopt the advice they came out with into your own life. (I did/do this often, for the record.)

This approach is comfortable. It feels better to indulge in how you *were* when you can place it in the context of how you are. It's closure. Most importantly, it's a story. **There's nothing satisfying about listing the ways you suffer and then leaving it without resolve.** People like transparency, but they don't like it without a little bit of blind optimism. Without hope, the story is too honest for comfort. Too much like real life.

Because this is as things really are: No matter how "good" your life is, there is always an open-ended list of ways you will inexplicably suffer without any real explanation. Whether you do it quietly or you let it bleed into other aspects of your life doesn't matter. This is our nature. You can do your best to distract or meditate or success it away, but suffering will always be present within happiness.

When I was approached to write about my life behind the screen, the parts of me that I usually keep private, my impulse was to do just this: to write about how I *was*, not how I am. I think that's the more interesting story, but it's not the one that's happening now. In lieu of no better cliché, I am a completely different person from the one I was three years ago. Of this, I am proud. **I have worked hard to be better. But that's all I am: better. Not complete.** It's not fair to you to just say how I've improved, and it's not fair to me to just list the ways I am still struggling. That feels like the cheap way out. The best I can do is just to weave together the truth of what life is really like.

I once read a story about a psychology professor who gave her students a lecture while holding a glass of water. They thought that the point of it would be something to do with the whole "glass half-full or half-empty" concept, but it wasn't. Her point was that the weight of the glass was nothing if she had to only hold it for a few seconds. In an hour, it would be hurting. If she had to do it for a whole day, her arm would be all but paralyzed by strain and she would be incapable of doing anything else. The point was that your mind is the same way.

I tell myself this often: "Put the glass down, Brianna."

I knew I had mental-health issues by the time I was in middle school, if not earlier. I did not think like the other kids did. I did not have the same emotional responses they did, either. The things that they found fun, I found stressful. Life was not inherently enjoyable for me, and I didn't understand why. This oddness has been my single most defining strength and my most unbearable weakness. In college, I finally went on medication for anxiety, depression, and OCD, but after taking it for a year longer than the psychiatrist recommended, I was stunned to discover that I was better, but I was not healed.

I am still not healed. There are still entire days that I just lie in bed and sleep. I overeat to numb myself. These feelings do not have an identifiable root cause— I have tried to fix and change every possible source they could be stemming from. **In some cases, I have been successful, and my life has transformed from those efforts.** But no matter how many things are "good," I am not excused from that human element. The harder I try to run and the better things get, the more acutely aware I become of how they could fall apart, of how they are impermanent. Though this usually passes as quickly as it comes, while it is with me

I am incapacitated for a bit. I have learned that these ebbs and flows are unavoidable but can be managed. **I know to be productive when I am feeling well, so I can collapse when I am not.**

I write for a living and I am used to speaking in a certain way. I present to you the pieces, and sometimes I am sure the shadow of what I am hiding is transparent. There is so much of this darkness that is laden through my writing. The bio on my Instagram says: "a semblance of the whole," and this is what I mean by it.

I once read a report that said that in antidepressant trial groups, most people given a placebo improved as much—if not more—than those given the real medication. The exceptions were the small percentage of those who were most severely ill. For them, the placebo didn't work. For them, just believing they are getting better didn't make them better. **When I am writing each day, I am doing it for that majority who can change their lives and heal themselves by just learning how to think differently. But I am in the group that may not get better, and I have chosen to believe that this is with purpose:** If I were to heal completely, I would not have to keep coming up with new solutions and ideas. The short of it is that I would not be able to help other people heal. So even on these very dark days, I remember that though this is a burden, I have made a way to use it as a gift. I do not mean to say that I am a martyr. **I am someone who has as much pain as anybody else but is willing to use it rather than run.**

Bios

Brianna Wiest is a writer, author, and editor. She edits Soul Anatomy and *Fine Living Lancaster* and writes for The Huffington Post, *Teen Vogue*, Thought Catalog, *Allure, Glamour*, and others. Her latest book, *101 Essays That Will Change The Way You Think*, is available now.

Chrissy Stockton is a writer, thinker, and creative cheerleader based on the Internet. She has a degree in philosophy and if she could have any superpower she would be able to talk to dogs. She is the author of *We Are All Just A Collection Of Cords*, a poetry book.

Sarah Lansky is a former philosophy professor and current producer at Zeus Jones in Minneapolis. She is a *Law & Order: SVU* anthropologist and coauthor of the book *PhiLOLZophy: Critical Thinking in Digestible Doses*, which was selected as a Kindle Single.

Kendra Syrdal is a writer and community manager at Thought Catalog. She's written all across the Internet for sites such as The Huffington Post, Grandex Inc, and BuzzFeed. She has published two books with

Thought Catalog. Currently, Kendra lives, laughs, and laments in Seattle with her dog and a bunch of succulents she's trying her hardest not to kill.

Sarah Bregel is a mother, a writer, a feminist, and a deep-breather based in Baltimore, Maryland. She has contributed to publications such as *The Washington Post, Good Housekeeping,* VICE, Vox, The Huffington Post, Babble, *Today*, The Daily Dot, Scary Mommy, The Establishment, *Parents, Fit Pregnancy, The Baltimore Sun*, and many more. Her essays have also appeared in multiple anthologies about motherhood and caregiving. She lives with her husband Marshall, their seven-year-old daughter Piper, and their two-year-old son Tener. Find her at Sarah-Bregel.com and on social media at facebook.com/sarahbregelwriter and @SarahBregel on Instagram and Twitter.

Mélanie Berliet is an Editorial Executive at Thought Catalog, where she gets to write about all sorts of stuff and do other super-cool things that make her happy. Previously, her work has appeared in *Vanity Fair, Elle, The Atlantic, New York Magazine, Cosmopolitan*, and many other publications. Also, she sucks her thumb. Still.

Ari Eastman is a poet, writer, feminist, and friend to all animals (except snails). Her work has been featured in Thought Catalog, The Rising Phoenix Review, and Words Dance Publishing. She currently works full-time as a staff writer for Thought Catalog and has published three poetry collections. She resides in California and would love to talk to you about *Buffy the Vampire Slayer* episodes.

Katie Sisneros earned her Ph.D. in English Literature from the University of Minnesota and currently works as the social media voice for Totino's. She is a founding co-editor of The Tangential, and previously her work has appeared in Paper Darts, Revolver, *Pif* magazine, Thought Catalog, and on Classical MPR. Her dog has kind of been annoying her lately.

Kim Quindlen is a staff writer and editor at Thought Catalog. She does improv and sketch comedy in Chicago. Her Uber rating is just okay.

Kaitlin Chappell Rogers is a newlywed, writer, Christian, friend, sister, recovering news reporter, and loud talker from Huntsville, AL. She's almost always late and loves to talk to strangers. Her most recent endeavors include being the most unorganized bride to ever live, becoming a yogi, and planting a garden. Her friends and family describe her as entertaining, extra, and essential. She cries a lot of happy tears because she's so thankful for said friends and family. She sleeps too late, talks too much, laughs too loud, and loves so big. You can find her and her blog at kaitlinchappell.com, facebook.com/kaitlinchappell-writer, and on Twitter and Instagram at @k__rog__. She loves new friends, so say hello!

Koty Neelis is writer and editor based in Chicago. Her work has been featured in VICE, Thought Catalog, and more. You can find her on Twitter at @sadgirlsocialclub.

Jen Kilgo is an author, truth-seeker, entrepreneuress, and ENFP who lives in Denver, Colorado, where she's still scared of pot because it once gave her a panic attack. She thinks best on airplanes and when upside down, and she believes that she can communicate telepathically with your dog.

Dana Bedessem is a strategist and co-manager of the Content Engine at Zeus Jones in Minneapolis. In a previous life, she launched startups in Silicon Valley and wrote online quizzes testing your shark IQ and questioning how [insert state] you really are. She's honored to be included alongside the talented women in this book.

Nikita Gill is a poet and graphic designer living in London, UK. Her book *Your Soul Is A River* is from Thought Catalog Books.

Katie Mather is a writer and editor at Thought Catalog. She lives in New York City, where she is almost always panicked about something.

Also Published by
Thought Catalog Books

Your Soul Is A River
Nikita Gill

101 Essays That Will Change The Way You Think
Brianna Wiest

Bloodline
Ari Eastman

We Are All Just A Collection of Cords
Chrissy Stockton

BROOKLYN, NY